I0827718

IMAGES
of America

Our Lady of Mount Carmel Italian Feast

Cousins Philip and Leonard Giangiulio lead the group of men carrying the statue of Our Lady of Mount Carmel in July in the early 1940s. This form of the Italian saint's day procession has changed little since its beginning. The procession and festival have become a valued sign of religious fervor in the community of Bridgeport. (Edith Barbone.)

On the cover: In the late 1940s, Our Lady of Mount Carmel Feast celebrations were joyous times. World War II had ended in victory for the United States, and many of Bridgeport's residents who served in the war were back home to take part in the processions. In 1947, when this photograph was taken, Fr. Joseph Megna had started a campaign to erect a new church on top of the existing basement church. That dream was realized on August 24, 1949, when the current church was dedicated. (Loretta Roscioli.)

IMAGES
of America

OUR LADY OF MOUNT CARMEL ITALIAN FEAST

Jack Coll and Maureen McQuaid

ISBN 978-1-5316-3673-9

Published by Arcadia Publishing
Charleston SC, Chicago IL, Portsmouth NH, San Francisco CA

Library of Congress Catalog Card Number: 2007937147

For all general information contact Arcadia Publishing at:
Telephone 843-853-2070
Fax 843-853-0044
E-mail sales@arcadiapublishing.com
For customer service and orders:
Toll-Free 1-888-313-2665

Visit us on the Internet at www.arcadiapublishing.com

Walking in the procession in the 1950s is a favorite memory for many Bridgeport children. The children all are dressed in their Sunday best. Rose DeStefano (the woman in the center of the photograph with the handbag) accompanies the young girls of the parish as they process from the school yard carrying the maypole. The maypole continues in use today. (Ann Amato.)

CONTENTS

Acknowledgments

Maureen McQuaid came up with the idea to honor Our Lady of Mount Carmel Church and the feast with an Arcadia publication that would include a few of the many thousands of pictures taken over the years of the church, school, and feast. Maureen felt it would be a great way to honor the many parishioners who have worked and attended the parish and the feast celebration over the past 83 years. Jack Coll was recruited by Maureen when he walked into the church rectory in search of photographs for another Arcadia publication. Maureen and Jack have worked very hard to meet Arcadia's high standards of producing photographs of interest, and they would like to thank the following contributors: Jim DeJoseph, who helped with much of the parish and feast information, as well as offering many photographs for consideration to this project; and Johnny Nicola and Paul Angelilli, who are no longer physically with us but whose spirit and lifelong love of this parish is evident in the many photographs and albums to their credit documenting so much of this faith community's history. Their legacy has proven to be invaluable. Please note that all photographs on loan for this project have a courtesy line, and the authors thank all contributors very much for their interest and contribution. Jack and Maureen would also like to thank the many people who contributed photographs that were not used in the book due to space limitations.

Rev. Salvatore J. Pronesti offered full support to the project and contributed throughout the process; without his help and encouragement, this book would not have been possible. Information for this book was provided by written church histories and information obtained from *Montgomery County: The Second Hundred Years* and the Norristown Boyd's directory.

Our Lady of Mount Carmel Church was founded in 1924, and the real credit for this publication is the thousands of volunteers who have contributed to the feast every year since its inception. A church is only as strong as its members, and Mount Carmel has had very dedicated volunteers for more than 80 years. Thank you all and may God protect you and bless you always.

INTRODUCTION

After World War I, there was a surge in Italian immigrants coming to the United States. They settled throughout the country but especially in the Northeast. The Norristown area attracted people from central and southern Italy and from Sicily. Since they were in a foreign country with a different language and very different customs and in an atmosphere that was often hostile, these immigrants felt the need to form societies for people with common bonds. Those bonds may have been based upon area of origin or allegiance to a patron saint. Societies with devotion to Our Lady of Mount Carmel are the most common in the United States. But there are others devoted to the Holy Savior, St. Valentine, La Madonna Grande, and La Madonna del Soccorso, as well as clubs for people from the same region.

The custom of celebrating the feast of Our Lady of Mount Carmel in Bridgeport had humble origins. The founding families began their observance of the feast with a religious procession through the streets and church services in their native tongue. Over the years, the celebration became more extensive. Entertainment for adults and children, homemade foods, and games of chance attracted more and more people to the celebration. Although the majority of the people attending the feast today are not of Italian origin or even parishioners, the life force of the feast rests in the numerous and devoted volunteers who mount the feast and work the stands for one reason—their love for our patroness, Our Lady of Mount Carmel.

—Rev. Salvatore J. Pronesti
Pastor of Our Lady of Mount Carmel Parish, Bridgeport (1994–present)

The Romanelli children pose for a family picture in the backyard of their home located at the corner of Seventh Street and Ford Street in Bridgeport on May 26, 1940. It was a special celebration with sisters Mary and Theresa both having made their first Holy Communion. (Nancy Buenzle Vietri.)

One

THE FOUNDING OF THE CHURCH

In the early 1920s, Bridgeport had trolley cars clanging along the tracks and hucksters set up on the busy street corners selling everything from food to footwear. James Bell was running his store on the corner of Holstein and Ford Streets from Monday through Saturday. On Sunday, Bell would rent his storage place and animal stable, located at 112 Holstein Street, to a group of Italian worshipers led by Rev. John Colantonio. Reverend Colantonio believed that the Italian group of worshipers could build a church, and on ground donated by Joseph and Philomena Phillips at the corner of Ford Street and Beech Alley, construction began on a basement church in 1924. The new parish was called Our Lady of Mount Carmel Church, and the rest is Bridgeport church history. (Armenti family.)

In 1982, Nicholas "Ace" Pagano presents Bishop Louis DeSimone with a plaque honoring him for being consecrated auxiliary bishop to the Archdiocese of Philadelphia. The presentation was made at the Knights of Columbus building at the 48th annual communion breakfast sponsored by Our Lady of Mount Carmel Church Holy Name Society. (Paul Angelilli.)

Mike Chendorain stands beside the Our Lady of Mount Carmel statue. This location later became the parish grotto area and is a favorite spot for people from the community to stop and reflect for a few moments. (Jim DeJoseph.)

The High Mass in honor of the patron saint is always very well attended. This shows the faith community participating at that mass celebrated by Fr. Edward Craney. The time is July 1981. The picture was taken from the choir loft and shows the interior of the upper church. (Jim DeJoseph.)

This 1973 photograph shows John DiBonaventure, Fr. Edward Craney (pastor of Our Lady of Mount Carmel), members of the clergy, and Jerry Nicola. The group is gathered outside the church waiting for the procession to commence. The neighboring parishes are always well represented. A priest from all the surrounding parishes usually joins in the celebration. (Our Lady of Mount Carmel Church.)

Over the years, the rectory has proven to be a pleasant area for many people to meet. Seen here from left to right are Johnny Nicola, Marion Mashintonio, Bishop Louis DeSimone, and Jerry Nicola sharing a few moments of conversation. (Rose Gentile.)

Shown here are the members of the Our Lady of Mount Carmel Mother's Club of 1959. The group includes, from left to right, (first row) Mary Rosiello, Marion Mashintonio, and Mrs. Leonard Berry; (second row) Rose Longo, Carmella Dieciedue, and Mary Messantonio. (Our Lady of Mount Carmel Church.)

Our Lady of Mount Carmel Church began in a rented building, a stable, and a storage place, and on August 9, 1924, the official establishment of the new Italian parish marked a new era in the small industrial borough known as Bridgeport. Just three weeks after opening ceremonies at the church, the very first wedding was performed. On August 31, 1924, Salvatore and Michelina DiNenna were the first couple to be officially married at Our Lady of Mount Carmel Church. The best man and maid of honor were Carmen Subranni and Carmela Dell'Angelo. The flower girl and ring bearer are unidentified. (Sal DiNenna.)

In 1979, upward of 500 Our Lady of Mount Carmel members and people from the community gathered at the dedication of the church grotto. Pictured from left to right are Joe and Frances Salamone, Tony and Carmella Alessandrini, and Gilda and Victor Cardone. Joe and Frances donated the St. Anthony statue that stands to the left of the grotto. Victor and Gilda donated the St. Gabriel statue that stands to the right of the grotto area. Tony gave unselfishly of his time during the entire construction of the grotto. He was the main engineer for the project. Also, credit must be given to Nunzio Falorio and his assistants Teodoro DiLullo, Joseph Acchione, and Nicola D'Angelo for their artistic work as stonemasons. The stones for the grotto came from a church in South Philadelphia and are over 300 years old. (Jim DeJoseph.)

In 1966, Fr. Edward Craney, pastor of Our Lady of Mount Carmel from 1955 until 1982, and Jerry Nicola, who served as the feast cochairman, as well as the general chairman for many years, stand by the statue of the parish's patroness as they discuss plans for the upcoming festival. The planning for the festival is a yearlong affair. (Our Lady of Mount Carmel Church.)

Fr. Joseph Amalfitano, third from the left, accepts a gift from Marion Mashintonio at a sodality reception held in June 1973. Other members attending the reception include, from left to right, Jerry Nicola, Anthony Valerio, Father Amalfitano, Mashintonio, Fr. Edward Craney, and Della Woyden. (Ronnie Mashintonio.)

Members of the Knights of Columbus Fourth Degree stand with the three DeSimone brothers (center). Fr. Russell, Fr. Salvatore, and Fr. Louis DeSimone (from left to right) were the sons of Antonio and Nicolina DeSimone, and all the family members belonged to the Our Lady of Mount Carmel parish. Russell, who studied in Rome, was ordained as an Augustinian priest in 1951. Salvatore studied at St. Bonaventure Seminary in New York and was ordained in July 1951. Louis was ordained in Philadelphia on May 10, 1952, and was consecrated as a bishop of the archdiocese on August 12, 1981. (Louis Paschall.)

Seen here are, from left to right, Emilio Roscioli, Anthony Differ, Esq., Rev. John Caulfield, and an unidentified speaker sharing a moment during the annual Holy Name Society father-and-son breakfast, which is held each year in March. (Our Lady of Mount Carmel Church.)

Members of the St. Valentine's Club located on Depot Street in Bridgeport are discussing plans for the society's participation in the Mount Carmel feast. From left to right are (first row) Carl Petrucci, unidentified, Joe Donofrio, and Anthony Saccomandi; (second row) Armondo Castellano, ? Messere, ? Donofrio, Salvatore Coscia, and Anthony Toro. (Our Lady of Mount Carmel Church.)

The St. Valentine lodge morra team is pictured here. Some of those present in the group include Joseph Messeri, Anthony "Chick" Chiccino, Gene Collilouri, Archangelo DelFiaco, Angelo Imperial, Pat Vance, Alex Fiorillo, Jerry Nicola, Sal Ruggiano, Tony Santucci, and Valentino Ottaviano. Morra is an Italian numbers game played with one's hands. (Our Lady of Mount Carmel Church.)

In support of the school programs, the women of the parish sponsored a mothers' fashion show. Seen in this fall 1963 picture are, from left to right, Theresa Damiani, Ann Amato, Lorraine Chendorain, Pat Coll, Theresa Ferreri, and Esther Bednar. (Theresa Ferreri.)

It is the early 1950s, and the ladies of the parish, along with Fr. Joseph Megna (far left), pastor, and Rev. John Caulfield (far right), assistant, line up around Santa to see what surprises he has. The women in the picture are, from left to right, Phil Paschall, Kate DeOrzio, Josephine Saccomandi, Margaret DeOrzio, Loretta Roscioli, Irene D'Ambrosia, and Mary Nicola. (Charles Paschall.)

Members of the 1995 Parish Pastoral Council meet in the dining room of the rectory to discuss upcoming events. Members include, from left to right, Joan and Anthony Saraceni, Francis Coscia, Sr. Mary Heffron, Marianne Wanczyk, Vince Mallon, Joe Kirk, Debbie Cane, Nick "Chief" Rotondo, Dave Fraschetta, Helen Desimone, and Ralph Bruno. (Our Lady of Mount Carmel Church.)

The members of the Blessed Virgin Mary Sodality gather for their monthly meeting in the school hall. Those in attendance are, seated from left to right, Fran Loghing, Dorothy Scandone, Theresa Proietto, Midge Fabrizio, Theresa DeStefano, Theresa Lawrence, Mary Ciaccio, Stella DiFillippo, Elsie Tancredi, Angie Grozinski, Clorinda Giangiulio, and Mary Costello. Standing from left to right are the 1995 sodality officers: Rose Dale, Ann Amato, Debbie Cane, and Ginny Pascale. (Our Lady of Mount Carmel Church.)

Principals at the 49th Mount Carmel feast annual two-day event back in 1973 include, from left to right, John DiBonaventure, feast cochairman; Rev. Raymond Tribuiani (affectionately known to many as "Father Ray"); Fr. Edward Craney, Our Lady of Mount Carmel pastor who was celebrant; Rev. Sante Piacente of the Don Guanella School in Springfield, Delaware County, who preached the sermon in Italian that year; and Jerry Nicola, who served as general chairman that year. (Our Lady of Mount Carmel Church.)

The sodality committee of Our Lady of Mount Carmel Church gathered for a meeting that included inducting new members in December 1960. Pictured from left to right are (first row) unidentified, Mary Lyczkowski, Mary Jo (Imperial) Dickinson, and unidentified; (second row) Rev. Arthur Centrella, Julie Nicola, Helen Desimone, Martha DiNenna, unidentified, and Marion Mashintonio. (Ronnie Mashintonio.)

Three good friends are seen here in this October 1996 picture taken in the Mount Carmel rectory. From left to right, Msgr. John Busco, Johnny Nicola, and Bishop Louis DeSimone share many happy memories of their days together at the parish. Monsignor Busco was an assistant priest at Mount Carmel in the late 1940s. He went on to become pastor of the Holy Saviour parish in Norristown. Nicola was a frequent and favorite visitor to the rectory. Bishop DeSimone was here to confer the sacrament of confirmation on 51 candidates that year. (Our Lady of Mount Carmel Church.)

On October 14, 1945, Alfred Spataccino and Connie Giangiacomo were married at Our Lady of Mount Carmel Church by Rev. John O'Connor. The happy couple is seen here as they leave the front steps of the church. Directly behind them are the best man and matron of honor, Lou and Josephine (Barone) Collins. With the end of World War II, there were a total of 33 weddings held at Our Lady of Mount Carmel from January through December that year. (Nancy Buenzle Vietri.)

Two

Early Feast Processions

In the 1940s, members of the San Salvatore Society pause to have their photograph taken while walking in the feast procession. They are seen here on Ford Street in front of Romanelli's Store carrying a statue of the society's patron saint, the Holy Savior. The three men standing in the front of the picture are father and son Natale and Salvatore Barbone and Larry DeStefano (to the Barbones' right). Directly behind DeStefano are Nick Iacovitti and Mike Barbaretta. On the left side behind Salvatore Barbone are, from front to back, Lou Ritrovato, Charlie Granese, unidentified, and Salvatore "Tootie" Pizza. (Bridgeport Hall of Fame.)

Children are seen walking up Ford Street during the feast procession in the 1940s. The young ladies holding the basket of flowers are cousins: Philomena (DeFusco) Barnhart (left) and Sue (DiSanto) Dayoc. The automobiles parked on the sides of the street have certainly changed over the years, but many of the residences pictured in the background have not. (Rose Dale.)

In the 1940s, children played a major role in the annual procession. Seen here on Prospect Avenue are Rose DeJoseph (Dale) front and center with Sue DiSanto (Dayoc) and Philomena DeFusco (Barnhart) behind her. At that time, the members of the church walked all over the town of Bridgeport. It was a welcome sight to many to finally return to the parish grounds for some rest and refreshment. (Rose Dale.)

Here is a very rare and early picture of the statue of Our Lady of Mount Carmel being carried in procession in 1940. These fine gentlemen are very respectfully dressed. Festivals like this one were the center of southern Italian religious life for many. For immigrants whose loyalty was not to the abstraction of Italy but to the village of their birth, the *festa* became an important symbolic link to their origins. The statue here appears to have a large amount of money pinned to it. In the early years, these monetary offerings were seen as a matter of family pride and devotion. (Edith Barbone.)

It is July 1953, and the president of the United States is Dwight Eisenhower. The vice president is Richard Nixon. And these young Girl Scouts from the parish are proudly marching in the Mount Carmel feast procession carrying their troop's banner and flag. Rita Palonicola and Grace Mallace are two of the girls pictured here. (Linda DeFrancisco.)

Members of the San Salvatore Society Club during the 1940s are seen here resting the statue on one of the tables a homeowner provided as a place of honor for the patron to sit on in a neighborhood. This would give people the opportunity to come forth and pray to the saint and offer a donation as well. The men who are standing guard by the statue are, from left to right, Matteo D'Ambrosia, Salvatore Barbone, John Iacovitti, John Palladino, and Mike DeStefano. (Edith Barbone.)

This photograph was taken in the school yard of the Our Lady of Mount Carmel parish showing young parishioner Salvatore DiNenna with assistant rector Rev. John Caulfield. DiNenna is wearing a costume depicting St. Salvatore, patron of Montella, Italy. The tradition of the children dressing as various saints and walking in procession continues today. (Sal DiNenna.)

The altar boys are taking over in this July 1953 procession picture. Angelo "Sonny" Armenti is leading the trio through the streets of Bridgeport. The man on the right is Frank Petrucci. (Linda DeFrancisco.)

Rev. John Caulfield, who was assigned to the Our Lady of Mount Carmel parish as an assistant to the pastor from 1948 to 1953, is seen here in the center of the picture. The procession appears to have come to a conclusion, and all are returning to the church grounds for the social to begin. Looking closely at the picture, one can see a Mobilgas sign in the background to the left. This was one of six gas stations in town at the time. (Edith Barbone.)

Both of these photographs show a representation of the feast procession in July 1955. In the photograph above, a group of young girls from the parish leads the way just in front of the banners depicting the societies represented in the parish at that time. And in the photograph below is Rev. Edward Iannucci, who was an assistant rector at Mount Carmel during the 1950s, walking in front of the group of men who were designated to carry the statue that year. In 1982, Reverend Iannucci returned to the parish assigned as pastor. He served the parishioners in that capacity until 1994. (Angie Cilio.)

The residents of Fifth Street in Bridgeport must have been thrilled to see the Our Lady of Mount Carmel procession pass by their homes in this 1940 picture. The parish festival and procession has always benefited by attracting the community of Bridgeport where those other than just Italians come out to celebrate Italianità in a pleasant small-town context. These good people from many years ago knew that it was important to keep the heritage strong and that it was also important to stay grounded in strong neighborhood ties. (Rose Valerio.)

Fr. Joseph Megna, pastor of Our Lady of Mount Carmel from 1940 to 1954, is seen here with Henry Churchill following close behind as they walk the path of the procession on Bush Street directly behind the church. Father Megna had already built two churches when he arrived in Bridgeport, but he decided to add to that list of accomplishments, and the upper church of the Mount Carmel parish came to be under his direction in 1949. (Jim DeJoseph.)

It is July 1970, and Anthony DiSanto Sr., Mike DeStefano, Salvatore Barbone, and Mike Barbone are seen carrying San Salvatore, the patron saint of the San Salvatore Society. The location here is Bush Street at the top of Seventh Street. (Sue Dayoc.)

Here are two of the original members of the San Salvatore Society, Gaetano Ritrovato (left), president of the club, and a Mr. Marsella. This society, as well as many others mentioned in this book, came into being as more people from a particular village immigrated to America. A few of the families would form a society to procure a statue, solicit contributions from *paesani* for music and celebrations, and re-create the procession in America that was very familiar to all from those areas in Italy. (Roseanne [Mardi] Kingkiner.)

The Bridgeport High School band accompanied the Our Lady of Mount Carmel parishioners as they honored their patroness in July 1940. Seen walking here on Prospect Avenue and providing the festival music are members of the band. This visible affirmation of support was displayed over the years by many from this close-knit town. (Rose Valerio.)

This 1940s faded photograph taken at the corner of Fraley Street and Hurst Street in town shows some of those who were interested in participating that year: a priest, Boy Scouts, a few men gathering to watch on the sidewalk, and a small child. (Edith Barbone.)

The annual procession is getting underway with the statue of Mount Carmel being carefully carried on Ford Street in July 1969. This is the core of the weekend celebration. (Shirley Bolognese.)

Crowds form outside the church. La Madonna Grande is coming down the steps in this July 1969 photograph. The Madonna is the patroness of families who originated in Fresa Grandinaria, Provinicia di Chieti. (Shirley Bolognese.)

It is July 1969, and these two little cuties walk with a float covered in flowers and ready for the festa. The small statue seen on the float is St. Theresa, and many people in the area have great devotion to her. She is the patron saint of flower growers and florists. An answer to a petition brought to this saint in prayer is said to be represented in receiving a yellow rose. (Shirley Bolognese.)

The children of the parish stand with the maypole on Ford Street in July 1969. The maypole is covered in the red, green, and white colors of a proper Italian festival. Notice the Cheerio Café in the background. The building was located across the street from the church at Fifth and Ford Streets. Over the years, the restaurant was also known as the Model "T" Tavern and the Burgundy Inn. (Shirley Bolognese.)

Madonna del Soccorso Society members, lead by Rudy DiGiacomo in the front left of the photograph, are seen carrying their patroness in procession. Virginia Verna is the woman credited with providing the beautiful jeweled cloak the statue is covered in. This statue sits in a place of honor in the lower church throughout the year. (Jim DeJoseph.)

The parish has always recognized that children are the future leaders in the church and the community in which members live and worship. They are the promise of a well-prepared faith force that will continue to draw people to the parish for many years to come. In this photograph are several children processing down Seventh Street following the flower-covered float with St. Theresa displayed on it. Lillian Colucci walks with her daughter Charlotte and many other little girls. (Sue Dayoc.)

Frank Bednar, Maria Palonicola, and Maria's sister, Lucia, are seen here on Fifth Street. A float carrying a statue of the Madonna is seen in the center of the photograph. Notice the Bridgeport Pharmacy in the background. The pharmacy, which began under the direction of Sal Coscia, had a soda fountain inside, and people often stopped in on warm summer afternoons for a freshly dipped ice-cream cone. They were the best in town! (Rita Chiccino.)

Ford Street in Bridgeport is always a busy place the second Sunday in July. The year is 1964, and Michele Roberto is preparing to walk in procession carrying a basket of flowers. As one can see, the many children in attendance are anxious for the festivities to get underway. (Michele [Roberto] Cantrell.)

Entertainment and music have always been important ingredients of every feast procession. Seen here are members of the Bridgeport High School band participating in the 1940s festival while marching along Fraley Street. (Edith Barbone.)

Members of the Knights of Columbus show good formation as they lead the Mount Carmel procession in 1973. Our Lady of Mount Carmel Feast, like the church, had very humble beginnings back in the 1920s. By the 1940s, the procession and surrounding events had grown, and by the mid-1940s, it became evident that the church had to grow from a basement church, so in August 1949, the completed upper church was dedicated. (Our Lady of Mount Carmel Church.)

In 1972, a song written and performed by Don McLean called "American Pie" was at the top of the music charts. *The Godfather* was the 1972 Academy Award winner at the movie theaters, and Fr. Edward Craney was in his 17th year of guiding Our Lady of Mount Carmel Church and was overseeing the 48th annual Italian festival. Anthony "Chick" Chiccino and John DiBonaventure lead the 1972 procession, carrying the Madonna down the church steps in preparation for the feast procession as parishioners look on. (Our Lady of Mount Carmel Church.)

The 1973 Our Lady of Mount Carmel Church procession was a hot and sunny one as Conshohocken mayor Francis Ruggiero (left), Bridgeport mayor Danny DeOrzio (third from left), and Norristown mayor John Marburger (fifth from left) all sport sunglasses as they lead the annual event. (Our Lady of Mount Carmel Church.)

Our Lady of Mount Carmel Feast has held a religious procession since 1924, and members who participate in the procession are always honored to be part of the church's proud tradition. Members of the Order of the Sons of Italy Valley Forge Lodge 1776 pose before marching in the 1973 procession. Standing in the center behind the banner is Bridgeport chief of police Joseph Collilouri, to the left of Collilouri is Rudy DiGiacomo, and on the right is Peter "Reds" Barbone. (Our Lady of Mount Carmel Church.)

Three of Our Lady of Mount Carmel's altar boys walk proudly in the feast procession in this 1940s picture taken in the vicinity of Fraley Street and Hurst Street. Seen are the cross bearer as well as the two boys carrying the candles. Up until the middle of the 1980s, only boys were allowed to act as altar servers. (Edith Barbone.)

Three

The School

In May 1963, Fr. Edward Craney, pastor of the parish, and his assistant, Rev. Arthur Centrella, are seen here seated with the parish's newest first communicants. Twenty-eight children are a part of this group and include Marlene Brandi, Joanne Ciacco, Charlotte Colucci, Debora Conti, Maureen DeStefano, Mary Falco, Sandra Giangiulio, Rosemary Longo, Anna Perone, Marie Valerio, Sheree Wadolny, Dennis Camarda, David Cavaliere, Louis Collins, John Denick, Russell Desimone, Salvatore DeSimone, Joseph Fabrizio, Thomas Ferreri, Samuel Franzone, Steven Gigliotti, Lawrence Granese, Joseph Loghing, Anthony Natalini, Stephen Rosiello, Ronald Sandor, Samuel Santoro, Charles Scandone, and David Tassoni. (Josephine Collins.)

This group of eighth-grade graduates hails from the Our Lady of Mount Carmel School class of 1965. Fran Augustine (third from right) and her girlfriends pose for this picture in the school yard on a very sunny day in June. Notice the school building in the background. The second floor, which is used to store all the feast equipment, has not been added at this point. (Jackie Alldridge.)

Here are five of the teachers who served the school in the 1950s. Standing in front of the school yard area are, from left to right, Sister Teracina Marie, unidentified, Mother Grace Mary, unidentified, and Sister Anne Louise. The Sisters of the Immaculate Heart order taught at the school from the opening year in 1952 until 2004. (Lorraine Strizziere.)

Here is a lovely pair, Angelo "Sonny" Armenti and his sister, Chris Armenti, all dressed up and having their picture taken in the school yard of Mount Carmel in 1953. (Linda DeFranciso.)

Confirmation day in March 1960 shows these three cousins, Joe Valerio Jr. and sisters Louise (center) and Janet Valerio, posing in their red and white gowns. All three were part of the class that year. With 177 children confirmed by Bishop Joseph McShea that day, it must have been quite a ceremony. (Rose Valerio.)

This photograph shows a pair of swell pals, Paul Angelilli (left) and his friend Dominic Toro. It is April 1954, and the picture was taken in front of the school yard on Ford Street. In the background is a clear image of the Cheerio Café, which was located directly across the street from the church. The former Tarlecki homestead was one of the oldest buildings in Bridgeport before it was razed in 1976. (Linda DeFrancisco.)

All dressed up in their first communion dresses, these young ladies are preparing to take part in the annual feast procession in July 1955. Jacqueline Augustine (third from right), along with the other girls shown folding their hands in prayer, waits in anticipation for her turn to begin the walk. Children from the first communion class are invited to participate each year and wear their outfits from their special day. (Our Lady of Mount Carmel Church.)

These three young girls are actually actresses in the eighth-grade school play in April 1966. Dressed rather convincingly as Immaculate Heart of Mary (IHM) nuns, the three classmates are, from left to right, Linda Shemar, Susan Picariello, and Donna Amato. Hopefully the teacher had a sense of humor about the choice in wardrobe! (Ann Amato.)

A classroom in the Our Lady of Mount Carmel School building often was filled to capacity with students, as seen in this shot of a 1950s class, which numbered on this picture day 42 pupils and one teacher. The last year the school was opened, there were just over 100 students from kindergarten through eighth grade, and the school was part of a consolidated school with the St. Augustine and Sacred Heart parishes and drawing students from all three. (Ronnie Mashintonio.)

It was a white jacket and bow tie affair as these young men file past the photographer in a state of reverence with their hands folded and their smiles on. The boys were all quite excited to be graduating from the eighth grade when this picture was taken on Ford Street across from the church in the 1950s. (Theresa Ferreri.)

Members of the first parish school graduating class on their special day in 1953 are seen here, identified from left to right as Angelo "Sonny" Armenti, Grace Mallace, unidentified, and Tony ?. A few sisters are also seen passing by in the background. (Linda DeFrancisco.)

An Easter basket for Mother Grace Mary is presented to her by Linda Angelilli in April 1954. They are standing on Ford Street in front of the rectory. It must have been a very cool Easter that year, judging from the coats everyone is wearing. (Linda DeFrancisco.)

This group of graduates reflects the last year Our Lady of Mount Carmel School existed on its own. Consolidation with St. Augustine School took place in September 1977. Members of the eighth-grade class of June 1977 are, from left to right, (first row) Lucia Boccella, Marilena Cieri, Barbara Santillo, Mary Pat D'Aprile, Anna Maffei, Theresa Cornacchio, Donata Paschall, Lisa Bello, Donna Crescente, and Lori Dougherty; (second row) Sister Immaculata, Rosa Addalli, David Rosa, Joseph Barajas, Jerry (Palonicola) Nicola Jr., Fr. Edward Craney, Robert Dayoc Jr., Onofrio Baldamenti, Robert Imperial, Salvatore DiGenova, Jean Pietluck, and Barbara Petrille. The new consolidation lasted until 1997. At that time, a further consolidation occurred, and along with Sacred Heart School in Swedesburg, the school became Holy Trinity Catholic School. Due to declining enrollment, the school closed in June 2005. (Sue Dayoc.)

The 1962 parish May procession is pictured here. (Josephine Collins.)

Members of the first communion class of 1959, Joe Valerio Jr. and his cousin Janet Valerio are pictured in the school yard. Both are dressed completely in white and looking quite saintly. (Rose Valerio.)

Seen here in 1972 are Patricia Woyden (left), Sister Miriam Cecelia, and Frances Gentile in the Our Lady of Mount Carmel School yard. (Rose Gentile.)

Janet Caramenico of Conshohocken stands with her fourth-grade class in October 1958 in the Our Lady of Mount Carmel School building. Caramenico was the first lay teacher to be hired by the school and began her career with teaching the children in the fall of 1956. She taught this same class; at that time the students were in second grade. (Philomena Roberto Johns.)

The May queen chosen as Our Lady of Mount Carmel School's first year came to an end was Mary Trigo. It is May 1953, and one can only imagine what a thrill and honor it must have been to be the one selected. (Linda DeFrancisco.)

Paul Angelilli poses with two of the sisters who taught in the school in 1953. (Linda DeFrancisco.)

The three bathing beauties pictured here are, from left to right, Rosemarie, Tiny, and Joan. They are enjoying themselves at the 1953 Mount Carmel school picnic. (Linda DeFrancisco.)

In May 1953, the members of the Our Lady of Mount Carmel girls' baseball/volleyball team pose together for a team picture across the street from Bridgeport Memorial Park. (Linda DeFrancisco.)

In 1962, Ronnie Mashintonio was selected as the "Sacred Heart Boy." Mary Rose Amato was the May queen that year. The young boys walking in front of Mashintonio seem to be led by one very jubilant gentleman. (Josephine Collins.)

It is first communion day in 1954, and a good-looking group of children has lined up to have its picture taken. All live in the same neighborhood, and all are part of the newest class of communicants at Our Lady of Mount Carmel. From left to right are Anthony Collins, Gregory Picard, Kathy Ross, Lorraine Collins, and Vivian DeStefano. (Josephine Collins.)

In June 1953, five of the graduates of the first-ever eighth-grade class from Mount Carmel and the principal, Mother Grace Mary, are standing in the school yard to the side of the rectory. (Linda DeFrancisco.)

Mother Superior Grace Mary and the crew pose for this picture in front of the school building in May 1954. The crew consists of Tony, "El Toro," and Sonny. (Linda DeFrancisco.)

Sister Patricia Anne, who taught first grade at the parish school in 1975, stands with the principal in the school yard. (Sue Dayoc.)

In November 1996, this group of Mount Carmel altar servers is getting ready for the confirmation to begin. The two girls in the group are Frances Hollup (third from left) and Alexis Strizziere (fifth from left). They are actually among the first of the girls to ever have served the parish in this capacity. Angelo DeLuca (far left) and Jimmy Ronca (second from left) are just two of the boys in the group. (Jim DeJoseph.)

Daniel Alldridge (right) and partner are leading the group of children who received their first communion from the church. The date is May 7, 1994, and 21 children made up the class that year. (Jacqueline Alldridge.)

The 2005 May procession finds the present pastor, Rev. Salvatore J. Pronesti, standing in the grotto area with four of the members of the first communion class. (Our Lady of Mount Carmel Church.)

This photograph of eighth-grade graduation in 1968 shows Tom Valerio standing with Sister Mary of the Infant in front of the school building. (Rose Valerio.)

Pictured here is the 1960 eighth-grade graduation with classmates and friends (from left to right) Lorraine Collins, Vivian DeStefano, Anthony Collins, and Greg Picard. (Josephine Collins.)

Here the May queen and her court are shown on the front steps of the church in 1953. The May queen is Mary Trigo. (Linda DeFrancisco.)

Our Lady of Mount Carmel School opened in September 1952 with an enrollment of 266 students in grades 1–8. This photograph was taken in 1957 of the fifth- and sixth-grade combined class. Within five years, the amount of students outgrew the school, and classes were held in the church basement. The teacher against the wall is Sister Mary Bridget, IHM. (Michele [Roberto] Cantrell.)

Frances (Franny) Gentile (right) and Cindy Powell are pictured here in this May procession during the 1970s. Beanies were always considered appropriate headwear for all Catholic schoolgirls at that time. (Rose Gentile.)

Four young men who graduated from the eighth grade and Mother Superior are pictured in 1953. (Linda DeFrancisco.)

Graduation ceremonies in 1977 brought these young people back to the parish for a special mass in honor of the best of the class that year. Shown with Rev. Raymond Tribuiani, standing from left to right are Michael DiSanto, Adele Armenti, Maryann DiSanto, Diane Orangers, and Lisa Biscotti. (Dolores DiSanto.)

Here in 1953 is the first graduating class of Our Lady of Mount Carmel School. Nine boys and girls make up the group. (Linda DeFrancisco.)

Mother Superior and the 1954 May queen are pictured here. (Linda DeFrancisco.)

Four of the first Immaculate Heart sisters who were assigned to Mount Carmel in Bridgeport pose for a photograph for the opening of the school in 1952. (Linda DeFrancisco.)

In May 1968, the annual May queen and her court are seen leaving the front of the church. (Shirley Bolognese.)

A first communion class poses in 1955. The two girls standing in the front of the group are Martha Chendorain and Marie Bolognese. Only 5 of the 53 children who were a part of the communicants that year are seen here. (Lorraine Strizziere.)

A quintet of graduates from the first graduating class is shown here in June 1953. (Linda DeFrancisco.)

Jim Costello, second in line, is a member of the 1963 eighth-grade graduating class from Our Lady of Mount Carmel School. He and other classmates are lining up for that final march. (Jacqueline Alldridge.)

Four

Church Events

In the 1940s, Alfonso and Rosa Romanelli and their children lived at the corner of Ford and Seventh Streets in Bridgeport. Pictured here are the Romanellis with nine of their children; their youngest son, born in 1946, does not appear in the photograph. They were a well-known and well-respected Mount Carmel family. The corner store they operated on their property for several years was a favorite shopping place for many of the town's residents. (Nancy Buenzle Vietri.)

It was a special time back in March 1982 when Bishop Louis DeSimone was the guest of honor at the 48th annual Our Lady of Mount Carmel Holy Name Society father-and-son communion breakfast. Bishop DeSimone, a member of the parish, attended grade school at the neighboring parish of St. Augustine in the late 1920s, long before Our Lady of Mount Carmel opened its school in 1952. In the photograph above are, from left to right, Fr. Edward Craney, Rudy DiGiacomo, Bishop DeSimone, and John Nicola. In the photograph below, from left to right are Jerry Nicola, Fr. Edward Craney, Bishop DeSimone, and Bridgeport police officer Deke Santillo. (Our Lady of Mount Carmel Church.)

"Friends for life" describes the two ladies pictured here. Rose Dale (above right and below left) and Emily Pires are found every year at the July feast working side by side in the pork and beef sandwich stand. In the photograph above, the girls are busy filling an order for a 2004 feast customer. Below they are posing in front of a home on Prospect Avenue in town dressed in their Girl Scout uniforms. The time is the early 1940s. They were members of the Our Lady of Mount Carmel Girl Scout Troop 222. (Rose Dale.)

In April 1953, Linda Angelilli (DeFrancisco) is looking rather cute and ready to begin her school day as she poses for this photograph on Ford Street in front of Our Lady of Mount Carmel School's yard. She was one of the 266 students enrolled in the first year of the school's opening. Notice the trees along Ford Street in the background. Today they no longer stand on the sides of the road but must have provided some pleasant shade on warm sunny days. (Linda DeFrancisco.)

Our Lady of Mount Carmel Boy Scout Anthony Collins is seen here in August 1957 standing with a companion in the backyard of his home. In the background, the family car is parked in the driveway. The average price of a home that year was $20,000. The average American production worker was making $82.32 a week. The cost of a gallon of milk was $1, gas was 24¢ a gallon, and a postage stamp was 3¢. (Josephine Collins.)

From left to right are Eagle Scouts John Cane, Ken Husar, and Keith Husar. The scoutmaster is Mike Santillo. In the back row, from left to right are Fr. Edward Craney, Sam Tassoni, John Lattanze, and Mayor Danny DeOrzio. Today John Cane is a sergeant with the Bridgeport Police Department. (Debbie Cane.)

Our Lady of Mount Carmel Boy Scout Troop 222 is shown here in the late 1960s. Standing at the left side of the group is John Cane; next to him is Ken Husar. Some of those also included in the picture are scoutmaster Mike Santillo, Kurt Husar, Ken Moravek, and Jimmy Burns. (Debbie Cane.)

Both Emilio and Loretta (Saccomandi) Roscioli were avid feast supporters and volunteered endless hours of their time, working the weekend of the festival for many years. They were two of the people instrumental in the months of planning that go into the successful event and were responsible for the financial accounting of the annual celebration. (Rose Dale.)

Here in this 1940s photograph are, from left to right, Nick Petrucci, Mick Ginonne, Larry Ruggiano, and Albert Mollica preparing for a special church outing. The buses have been chartered, and the men are all well dressed as they wait patiently for the rest of the group to arrive. Flowers adorn all four gentlemen's lapels. (Rose Valerio.)

Tonino Gaeto and his daughter Mary are seen standing in front of the World War II honor roll, which was located in the yard to the right of the Our Lady of Mount Carmel rectory. The little girl with her back to the camera is Sandra Gaeto. The honor roll served as a tribute to all the Bridgeport sons and daughters serving their country during World War II. The list grew to include more than 400 Bridgeport residents who served in the war from 1941 through 1945. (Jim DeJoseph.)

Members of the Our Lady of Mount Carmel parish gather outside the church following a mass in honor of their patroness. The statue can be seen in the background as the men prepare to carry it in procession. Some of those in the photograph include a Mrs. Paciello, George and Emilio Roscioli, Nick Ivone, a Mrs. Pizza, and Tony Santillo. (Rose Valerio.)

This event, which appears to take place at Valley Forge Park in 1965, shows Boy Scout Thomas Ferreri from Our Lady of Mount Carmel Boy Scout Troop 222 earning a badge. Through the years, Scout troops have been an important ingredient for the young people of the parish to help build character. (Theresa Ferreri.)

In April 1964, this group of Cub Scouts from the Our Lady of Mount Carmel parish must have been thrilled to meet with boxing champion Joe Ciardello. The den mothers included in the picture are Rose Valerio, Mary Ross, Grace Carfagno, and Carmel Gininni. (Rose Valerio.)

In 1961, *West Side Story* was adapted for the big screen and went on to win an Oscar for best picture. Patsy Cline released "I Fall to Pieces" and "Crazy." The songs helped her to cross over from country to pop. And Martha Chendorain, who is seen in this photograph with her mother, Alice, is graduating from the eighth-grade class of Our Lady of Mount Carmel School in Bridgeport. (Lorraine Strizziere.)

It is May 1940, and Mary and Theresa Romanelli are celebrating their first communion day with their father, Alfonso, and their younger sister. There were 57 first communicants that year at the Our Lady of Mount Carmel parish. The members of the Romanelli family were all active participants of the parish for a many years. Alfonso, who died on April 6, 1980, is buried at St. Augustine Cemetery. His gravestone features a nearly life-size image of Our Lady of Mount Carmel. (Nancy Buenzle Vietri.)

This 1992 picture shows two good friends, John Nicola (right) and Paul Angelilli, standing on the DeKalb Street bridge. In the background is a billboard advertising the upcoming Italian festa. Always interested in reporting and photographing events surrounding the feast, the two no doubt are discussing plans for the annual event. (Our Lady of Mount Carmel Church.)

Celebrating the 2005 feast are, from left to right, Bishop Michael Burbidge, the main celebrant of the feast mass; Fr. James Shea; Sue Dayoc; and Rev. Salvatore J. Pronesti, pastor of Our Lady of Mount Carmel Church. Bishop Burbidge was a former student of Father Pronesti's. Father Pronesti taught at Cardinal O'Hara High School in Springfield before his assignment to Bridgeport. Bishop Burbidge was named an auxiliary bishop of the archdiocese in 2002. (Our Lady of Mount Carmel Church.)

In April 2000, the Our Lady of Mount Carmel parish celebrated its 75th anniversary with a banquet held at the Presidential Caterers in East Norriton. On August 9, 1924, the Our Lady of Mount Carmel parish was officially established, and within a year and a half, the church population had grown to more than 1,200. Anthony (Tony) Bolognese and Edie Barbone are enjoying themselves dancing at the anniversary as Mary Messantonio is seen dancing in the background. (Our Lady of Mount Carmel Church.)

At the parish's grand celebration for its 75th anniversary in 2000, George "Chendy" Chendorain and Fr. Raymond Tribuiani are seen in this photograph sharing a good laugh. The affair was a culmination of a year of special events held in recognition of this important milestone. (Our Lady of Mount Carmel Church.)

Bishop Louis DeSimone attended the Our Lady of Mount Carmel 48th annual Holy Name Society father-and-son communion breakfast in 1982. Bishop DeSimone grew up on Ford Street in Bridgeport and attended Bridgeport High School. In 1952, DeSimone was ordained a priest and celebrated his first mass at his home parish. In the photograph above, Bishop DeSimone is flanked by Paul Angelilli (left) and Dominic Lasorda. In the photograph below, from the left to right are Tony Gaeto, Peter "Reds" Barbone, Joseph Bearoff, Bishop DeSimone, Beef Mattiola, and Connie Eliff. (Our Lady of Mount Carmel Church.)

It appears to be a warm summer day in 1969 as Sister Frances Anthony stands with a group of ladies from the parish. From left to right are Rose Gentile, Minnie Pagano, Sister Frances Anthony, and Della Woyden. The statue of Our Lady of Mount Carmel is behind the ladies. This statue is now the center point of the parish grotto. Children can also be seen playing in the school yard behind the four women as the photograph was taken. (Rose Gentile.)

Here is a very important group of men. The collection counters for Our Lady of Mount Carmel Church take time out to salute (not while they are counting, of course) in May 1968. From left to right are John DiFillippo, John Palumbo, Fr. Edward Craney, Joseph Russo, and Ralph Bruno. Ralph Bruno not only continues as a weekly counter as of 2007 but is the annual feast ground coordinator. He oversees the setup of the three-day weekend operation and the cleanup that follows. (Our Lady of Mount Carmel Church.)

The community of Our Lady of Mount Carmel came together many times in happy celebration. Here in the 1980s are, from left to right, Paul Angelilli, Bishop Louis DeSimone, and Mary Bacchi enjoying a party honoring Fr. Edward Craney for his years of pastoral services at the Mount Carmel parish. Father Craney remains one of the most beloved priests to ever have taken up residence in the town of Bridgeport. (Our Lady of Mount Carmel Church.)

At the Presidential Caterers in 2000, this is the group of eucharistic ministers who served in this ministry during the 75th anniversary year. The group poses on the beautiful staircase at the banquet facility. Those included are, from left to right, (first row) Charlotte Iannone, Dora Rossi, Connie Capaldo, and Maureen DeOrio; (second row) Sue Dayoc, Basil Iannone, Michael Savo, Bob Wagner, and Dolores DiSanto; (third row) Debbie Cane, Mark DeOrio, Lou Slutz, Geraldine Pizza, and Vince Mallon. (Our Lady of Mount Carmel Church.)

Five

Feast Processions in Recent Years

In this 2006 photograph, Giammarino DiGiuseppe, also known as Jim DeJoseph, poses with his two great-granddaughters, Georgia and Giovanna Cwienk, inside the school cafeteria. Each year, the children who plan to join in the procession gather here prior to the beginning of the annual walk. Georgia (left) and Giovanna are dressed and ready to go. They are becoming regular attendees. Their great-grandfather is a lifelong feast volunteer. He helped construct the original cherry carrier that was used in the procession each July to carry the statue of Our Lady of Mount Carmel through the streets of Bridgeport by members of the Congrega Society. In recent years, he was instrumental in designing the steel cart that the statue now rests upon during the procession. The cart has been seen as a godsend to those who have carried the statue, which weighs well over 600 pounds. (Jim DeJoseph.)

In this 1990 picture, the procession makes its way down Ford Street. Some of the members of the Congrega Society who are carrying the statue and walking alongside include Jerry Nicola, Carmen Scandone III, John Nicola Jr., Sam Franzone, Darryl Bacchi, and Jim DeJoseph. In the background, the community support is evident as seen by the flags on top of the church as well as the flags on the telephone poles, which are put in place each year with the help of the Borough of Bridgeport and the local firehouses. (Our Lady of Mount Carmel Church.)

As the procession continues to make its way up Bush Street, which runs directly behind the church grounds, a few new faces are seen. Joe Valerio is ready to take his turn at the front left of the statue. Because of the weight of the carrier and the statue, it took quite a large group of devotees to make their way through the entire procession route. (Our Lady of Mount Carmel Church.)

It is July 1981, and the sun is surely sticking with this group of youths from Our Lady of Mount Carmel Church as they begin to carry a small model of the church's namesake during the 57th annual celebration. (Our Lady of Mount Carmel Church.)

For those who live in Italian American communities, festival time can feel almost like Christmas. Here are three young ladies on a beautifully decorated float. It is tradition that one child each year wear the Mount Carmel costume. The girls who are chosen to ride with her each receive bouquets and headpieces made of the freshest, most fragrant flowers. This is always an honor and great thrill for the children who are selected. (Our Lady of Mount Carmel Church.)

Men, women, and children all form the group of St. Valentine Society devotees as they accompany their patron saint on Ford Street in Bridgeport during the July 1990 feast. Seen in the background is a very popular delicatessen that was operated for many years by Frank and Jean Aquilante, Frank's Cold Cuts. Frank and Jean, members of the Our Lady of Mount Carmel parish, were always generous in their donations to the festival. (Our Lady of Mount Carmel Church.)

In 1982, Amerigo Cieri and friends proceed to carefully carry the statue of St. Valentine on Bush Street by the corner of Rambo Street. (Our Lady of Mount Carmel Church.)

The Our Lady of Mount Carmel statue with flowers galore surrounding the bottom of the base is carried from the front of the church in July 1981. From left to right, Anthony "Chick" Chiccino, Jim DeJoseph, and Mike Chendorain are all long-standing members of the church's Congrega Society. (Jim DeJoseph.)

This scene on Ford Street in 1980 shows some of the local community supporters as well as the mayor of Hammonton, New Jersey. From left to right are Nicholas "Ace" Pagano, the mayor of Hammonton, Steve Tomchick, Bridgeport mayor Danny DeOrzio, and chief of police Joe Daloisio. Directly behind the group are members of the Knights of Columbus preparing to march in the procession. To the right of the group is the sign for Puco's Market, a very popular store for a number of years in the borough. (Our Lady of Mount Carmel Church.)

Leading this group of children in the July 1981 feast procession on Ford Street are Leslie Hanna (left) and Maria Palonicola. First communicants dressed in their finest follow closely behind. Parish children who receive their first Holy Communion in May each year are always invited to participate in the annual procession. (Jim DeJoseph.)

It is 1980, and women from St. Michael's parish in Germantown join in the procession. They are all part of the Madonna del Soccorso Society. The parish was closed in 1982, and Rev. Edward Iannucci, the pastor of Our Lady of Mount Carmel, granted the group permission to keep their statue in Bridgeport. It can be found year-round in the lower church, safely encased in a glass enclosure. (Jim DeJoseph.)

Marching in the 1981 Our Lady of Mount Carmel religious procession are, from left to right, three borough mayors: Mayor John Marburger of Norristown, Mayor Francis Ruggiero of Conshohocken, and Mayor Danny DeOrzio of Bridgeport. In the center of the photograph are Montgomery County sheriff Fred Hill, Joe Interrrante, and Bridgeport police sergeant Deke Santillo. The 1981 feast was highlighted by Sunday evening fireworks at the conclusion. (Our Lady of Mount Carmel Church.)

This wonderful photograph taken in the early 1950s shows the procession heading in a different direction than people are accustomed to today. Heading up Ford Street is Rev. Domenic Grande, a missionary priest who often preached the High Mass held in honor of Mount Carmel in Italian. The altar boys who accompany him are Jerry Nicola (left) and Lou Paschall. Directly behind Father Grande is Francis (Frankie) Iacovino. Some of those carrying the statue include Pierino Veramonti, Anthony DiSanto Sr., Dominic Toro Sr., and Louis and Angelo "Gus" Diana. The man at the far left of the picture is Antonio DeSimone, and walking on the sidewalk is Harry Antonelli. Many of the banners shown in this picture are still in use today. (Our Lady of Mount Carmel Church.)

Anthony Shepperd is preparing to lead the way in 2004 with two members of the first communion class on either side. Behind them is a group of children being instructed by their well-meaning mothers as to how to manage the maypole. Also seen is the Lafayette Ambulance Squad parked to the side of the group. The presence of the ambulance and its well-trained crew members lends a sense of security to the entire weekend of the feast. (Our Lady of Mount Carmel Church.)

Children are always an important part of the procession. Seen here are Christina Capaldo, Danielle Conway, and Rachel and Samantha Morrison, to name just a few, looking quite pleased to be a part of the 1998 festival. (Our Lady of Mount Carmel Church.)

Carmelina (Churchill) Edwards, on the right, gives instructions on carrying the small statue of Our Lady of Mount Carmel in the annual procession. Edwards was born on July 16, which is the feast day for Our Lady of Mount Carmel, thus her name in honor of Mount Carmel. (Our Lady of Mount Carmel Church.)

Pictured here is the 1990 procession on Bush Street. The gown and veil that cover the statue were made by Palma Pizza Ottaviano in honor of her devotion to the patroness. (Our Lady of Mount Carmel Church.)

The procession is underway following the noon mass with the presentation of the St. Salvatore statue. Anthony DiSanto Sr. is on the left, Richard Ritrovato is seen balancing the statue in the center, and Sal Rotondo can be found on the right. (Jim DeJoseph.)

Brothers Vince and Pat Gazzillo, who are strong supporters of the parish and are always participants in the annual procession, are seen here walking in this 1980s July photograph. The brothers have great devotion to St. Pio and in recent years have donated a statue of the saint to the parish. This is the newest statue to be carried in the procession. (Our Lady of Mount Carmel Church.)

A large group of the St. Valentine Society is seen here on Bush Street in July 1981. Its lodge is located on Depot Street in Bridgeport. (Our Lady of Mount Carmel Church.)

Schoolchildren are ready to participate in this 1978 photograph. Pictured are Tracy Cipriano, Nikki Piermatteo, Gina Rulo, Mary Rose Chiccino, Carol Vanzzandt, Noelle Rotondo, Maria Santoro, Anne Hunsicker, Nadine Rotondo, Melissa Wtulich, Joseph Inzone, Debbie Crescente, Phyllis Meoli (who has charge of the group), Bernadette Volpi, Kim Veramonti, Mark Santoro, Becky Wheeler, Lisa DiSpirito, Andrea Granese, and Maribeth Giannone. (Rita Chiccino.)

The children carrying the small statue pose in front of the grotto just before heading back into the church. Wearing ties, Aldo Sciarrino, Carmen Pino, Nick Chiccino, and Darryl Bacchi all stand behind the group to lend any needed support in 2003. (Our Lady of Mount Carmel Church.)

Members of the living rosary are shown in procession in this 2004 photograph on Bush Street. The group includes Domenick Martino, who leads the recitation of the rosary, Sue Dayoc, Linda Korpel, Edith Barbone, Francesco and Josephine DiRubbo, and Frank and Gabriela Raffa. The rosary is actually made up of the individuals who chose to walk. (Sue Dayoc.)

This is one of the happiest sights of the day for the many who gather to watch the procession. In this July 2000 picture, the men from the parish are seen carrying the patroness high on their shoulders. Darryl Bacchi is helping to safely direct his fellow Mount Carmel members as they make their way on Ford Street. Holding the statue are Joe Kirk on the front left and Wayne DeMitis on the right front, and Anthony Chiccino and Nicky Douigerakis are behind DeMitis on the right. (Our Lady of Mount Carmel Church.)

Rev. Salvatore J. Pronesti, the sixth pastor of the parish, is seen here following the annual feast mass. His vestments reflect the patroness, Our Lady of Mount Carmel. (Our Lady of Mount Carmel Church.)

Each year the community of Bridgeport allows Our Lady of Mount Carmel to proceed with the annual plans for the festa. Here are two of the members of the St. Salvatore Society, Attilio Bolognese and Jerry Kubrinski (left), leading some of the borough's finest down Ford Street in July 2000. The town officials include Bridgeport police chief Zenny Martyniuk, Mayor Thomas Novitski, and Judge Jack Kowal. (Our Lady of Mount Carmel Church.)

It is July 2000, and seen here are the ladies who make up the members of the Madonna Grande Society gently guiding the patroness on her way in procession. Ninetta Toro makes sure the Madonna's veil is properly positioned and the skirt on the cart is pristine each year. (Our Lady of Mount Carmel Church.)

Carmen Pino (right) and Nick Chiccino hold the statue as it is turned in the direction of a devotee in need of extra prayers. This is a tradition that originated in the small towns of Italy. (Our Lady of Mount Carmel Church.)

Vince Iacavino and Pat Cardone are just two of the dedicated members who walk with the patron of the St. Valentine Society each year. The pride and devotion they display is evident on their faces at each procession. (Our Lady of Mount Carmel Church.)

Pictured here are members of the Verdi Band from Norristown. The band was first established in 1920, and for many years, it has provided the musical journey to accompany those who march in procession. (Our Lady of Mount Carmel Church.)

During this 1990s feast, the clergy is well represented. Msgr. Charles Vance, Msgr. John Marine, Rev. James Shea, Rev. Salvatore J. Pronesti, Rev. Joe Zingaro (Sacred Heart in Swedesburg), and Msgr. Francis Schmidt (St. Augustine in Bridgeport) are seen here from left to right. (Our Lady of Mount Carmel Church.)

Sisters Jenna and Alexandra (Lexie) Bednar are seen here in the Our Lady of Mount Carmel School cafeteria just prior to the start of the July 2005 procession. Jenna has the honor of being dressed as the patroness. Her sister will walk with her with her headpiece made of flowers and her bouquet. (Our Lady of Mount Carmel Church.)

There are only smiles on the faces of the 2002 members of the Order of the Sons of Italy Valley Forge Lodge 1776 as they join together as a group for this photograph. Seen here on Ford Street on this beautiful July day are, among others, David Tassoni, Armand Barbone, and David Carmenico. The Sons of Italy are always wonderful supporters of the annual festival. (Our Lady of Mount Carmel Church.)

Comfortable footwear is in order for these youngsters as they make their way with the maypole along Bush Street in Bridgeport. (Our Lady of Mount Carmel Church.)

The wind is beginning to blow slightly, as can be seen in the statue's veil. Seen just behind the statue is the former Bridgeport High School, which was demolished in 2001 to make way for 30 town houses. Those carrying the statue include Nick Chiccino, Carmen Pino, Jamie Strizziere, and Vince Mallon. Walking alongside the group are John Capaldo, Lou Slutz, Aldo Sciarrino on the right, and Joe Valerio and Michael Savo can be found on the left. (Our Lady of Mount Carmel Church.)

Six

FEAST CELEBRATIONS

Salute! From left to right, George "Chendy" Chendorain lends his assistance to Willie Messantonio, with Angelo DelFiacco and Reds Biscotti standing by. These four gentlemen seem to have the festivities well in hand. (Jim DeJoseph.)

Restocking the stands with food and supplies is a never-ending task the weekend of the feast. Seen here are Edie Barbone and Basil Iannone at the 2004 celebration. Ordering and preparing the food and setting up the stands is a major undertaking each year as hundreds of hours are spent leading up to the annual event. (Our Lady of Mount Carmel Church.)

Ralph Bruno and Msgr. Arthur Centrella are happy to wait for their delicious sausage sandwiches. Both have shared many years together here at Our Lady of Mount Carmel. Bruno is a lifelong member and actively participates in many activities the parish offers. Monsignor Centrella was assigned here as an assistant priest in the 1950s. He has returned every year in July and is one of the most ardent supporters. (Our Lady of Mount Carmel Church.)

It is 1984, and having some terrific festival fun are Michael and Christine Stackhouse. They are sharing a swinging amusement ride on the grounds of the church. Through the years, the rides have always been a favorite of the younger visitors. (Our Lady of Mount Carmel Church.)

In this 1980s feast version of *Wheel of Fortune*, many of the local neighbors wait anxiously to see who the winner is. The faces in the crowd include Billy Cox, Dave and Maria Norman, Toni and Angie Boccella, and Sal DeMarco. Games of chance are plentiful on the grounds the weekend of the festival. (Our Lady of Mount Carmel Church.)

Floyd and Diane Pachella are happy to greet the many players who navigate toward the Whiskey Wheel each year. This stand is supplied by donations made by Mount Carmel parishioners and friends. Winners are very happy to walk away with a bottle of cheer of their choice for only 50¢ a spin. Warning: no one under the age of 21 may play! (Bill Ross.)

Via Veneto water ice is served up to the crowds by these three smiling young ladies. From left to right are Fran Loghing, Debbie Cane, and Phyllis Melasecca. All three are veteran feast workers. On a warm July evening, nothing tastes better than this delicious treat. (Our Lady of Mount Carmel Church.)

From left to right, Dominic Ranieri, Angelo DeLuca, and Vince Giangiulio are seen in this vintage 1950s picture. These three friends are the original sausage stand team. They are preparing the sausages in a tabletop grill, and according to the sign, one can purchase a sandwich for 50¢. Today those sausage sandwiches are $4. (Angie DeLuca.)

Many of the booths at the annual Mount Carmel festival have entire families working them, as was the case back in the mid-1990s when Connie Pizza (left) worked with her son-in-law Bob Wagner, who is standing next to Lou Carfagno and Connie's husband, Joe Pizza, on the end. All are sporting the official feast worker pin and wearing the official colors of red, white, and green. (Bill Ross.)

Our Lady of Mount Carmel Feast has been operating for 83 years with the help of volunteers like Stephanie Dippollito (left), Sue Dayoc (center), and Ginny Pascale. Dayoc and Pascale have volunteered at the feast their entire lives. (Our Lady of Mount Carmel Church.)

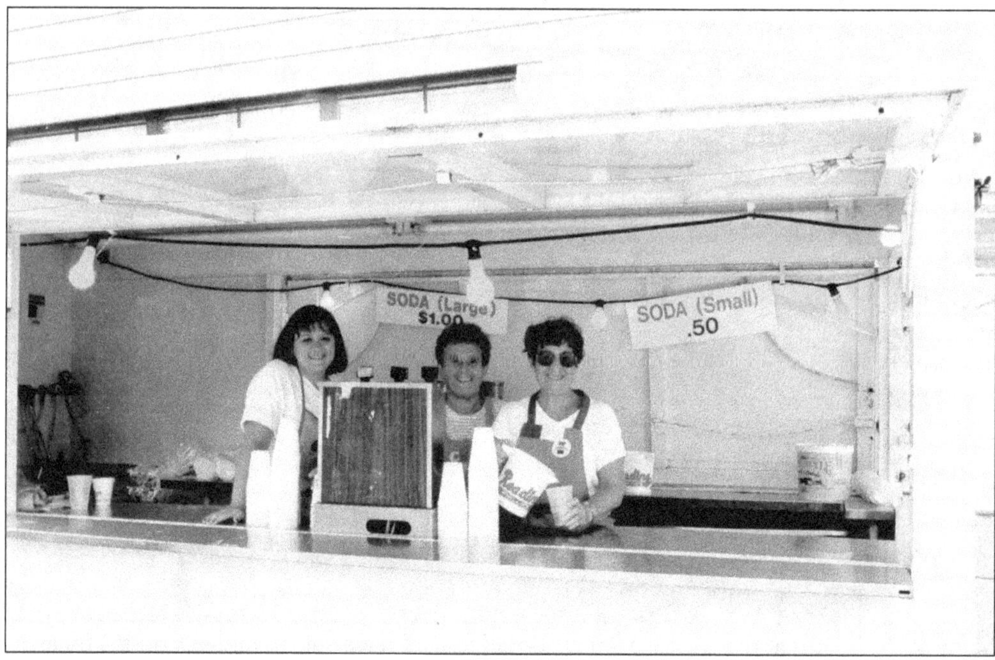

Three very pleasant ladies work hard to be sure no one leaves the feast thirsty. Ann Amato along with her sister Rita Granese and her niece Amy can be seen in this July 2000 photograph standing in the soda truck waiting for their next customer to step up. (Our Lady of Mount Carmel Church.)

A hardworking group of volunteers takes a break at one of the busiest stands during the 1998 feast weekend. Included in the group are Enis Praskay, Christine Chendorain, Carol McDevitt, and Helen Trecroce. The fried dough is without a doubt at the top of favorite foods at the feast. (Our Lady of Mount Carmel Church.)

Lifelong residents of Bridgeport and members of the Our Lady of Mount Carmel parish can be seen working the Treasure Trove stand during the feast. The Treasure Trove is a popular spot during the weekend for visitors looking to take a chance on winning baskets filled to the brim with gift certificates and other goodies. Local businesses and individuals contribute to the contents of each basket. Rosemarie (Ottaviano) Slutz is seated in the chair, and Jacqueline (Augustine) Alldridge is behind her. Both have volunteered at the feast for years. (Our Lady of Mount Carmel Church.)

Behind-the-scenes work seems never ending, especially to the three sisters who make the dough that supplies the *pizza fritta* (fried dough) stand for the entire three-day weekend. Above, Celeste Wheeler (left) and Maria Skaw seem very happy as they gently knead the dough. Below, Carol McDevitt adds a little more milk to the giant mixer that churns out buckets of dough for the feast. With 2,000 pounds of flour and 250 pounds of sugar used each year, it is a wonder these three ladies are seen outside the kitchen at all each July. (Our Lady of Mount Carmel Church.)

Jerry Scandone, shown here, along with his wife, Paula, and children, Lauren and Justin, has coordinated and run the chicken finger stand since 2001. Jerry brings his warm sense of humor and his unique and invaluable experience in the food service industry with him each year as he helps the church conduct another successful event. (Frank Pronesti.)

The Treasure Trove gets better and better every year. Nicole DeLuca and Ryan Conboy are much-appreciated assistants of Anna Mae Daloisio as the 60-plus baskets are brought out and set up for all to enjoy. Chances are sure to go fast as people try to choose which one of the many gifts they would like to win. (Our Lady of Mount Carmel Church.)

By 1984 when this photograph was taken, more that 12,000 visitors over the three-day feast period in July were part of the annual Mount Carmel celebration. Harry Shultz holds his three-year-old grandson Frankie Shultz, who is holding a stuffed animal he won at the Animal Wheel. Festival volunteers include Emidio Rosa (left) and Lou Paschall (right). (Our Lady of Mount Carmel Church.)

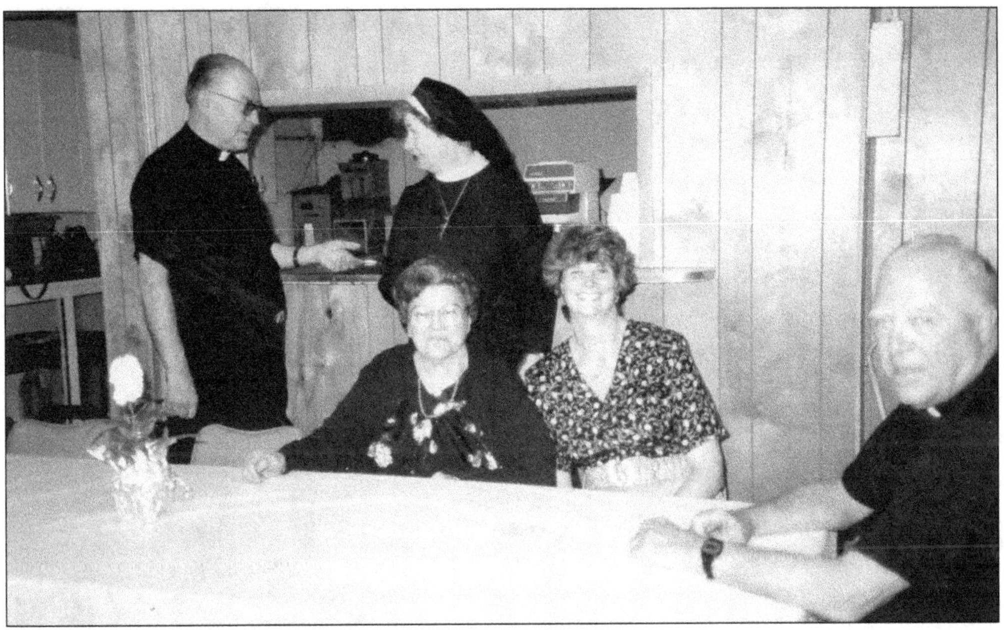

In this 1991 picture, Marion Mashintonio (seated left) and Debbie Cane are enjoying themselves at a luncheon in honor of Mashintonio's 26 years as Blessed Virgin Mary Sodality president. Cane was selected to succeed Mashintonio as the new head of the sodality. Fr. Francis Donovan, a resident priest at the parish, looks on. In the background are Rev. Edward Iannucci, pastor of Our Lady of Mount Carmel, and Sister Anne Christine, who is the principal of the parish consolidated school. (Rose Dale.)

Pictured here are Marion Mashintonio (seated center) and her sisters, Louise DeJoseph (left) and Theresa Lawrence standing behind her. Lawrence and DeJoseph are lending their support to Mashintonio, who is being recognized for her years of commitment to the Blessed Virgin Mary Sodality group. All three have worked at the feast since they were children. Happy times are always plentiful at Mount Carmel's celebrations, and these ladies certainly add to the enjoyment. (Rose Dale.)

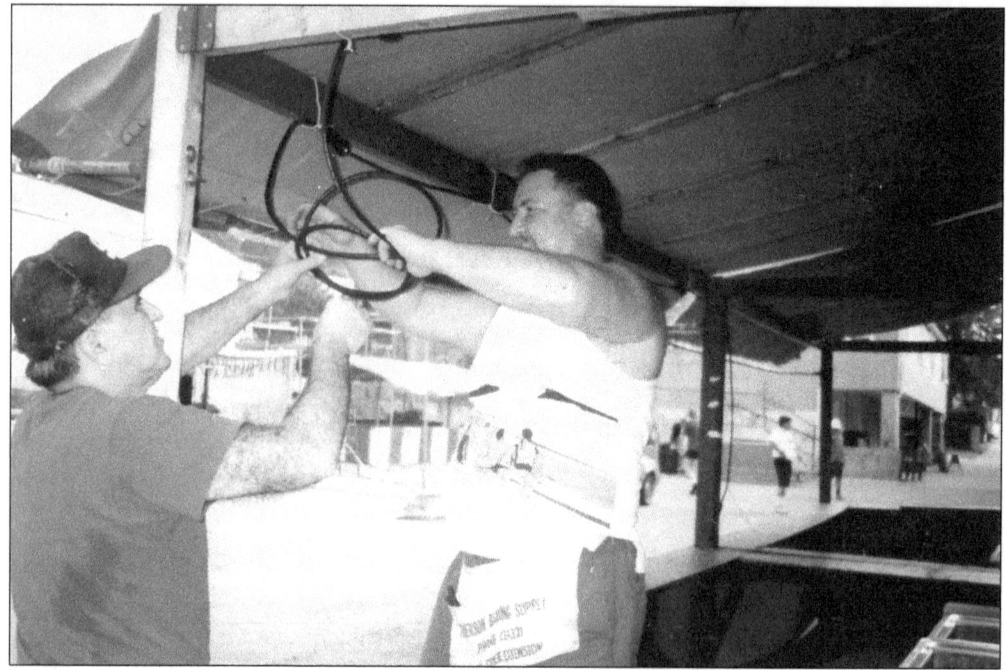

In 1993, as occurs every year, teamwork is evident everywhere one looks. Nick "Buddy" DeRosato (right) and Anthony (Tony) Natalini are well underway with the electrical work. The two are connecting the food stands with lighting so once nighttime falls on the feast area everyone would be able to see. (Rita Chiccino.)

Two long-enjoyed festival treats are *la trippa* and *suffrito*, which is being served with a smile by, from left to right, Peggy Logan, Gloria Mastrocola, and Ginny Pascale. (Our Lady of Mount Carmel Church.)

Hard at work at the 2000 festival are, from left to right, Alexis Strizziere, Lauren Edwards, and Lorraine Strizziere, all standing in the front of the booth. Standing and cooking in the back of this photograph is Denise Davis, and to the side of the stand is Maureen DeOrio. (Our Lady of Mount Carmel Church.)

The three happy faces shown in this late-1990s picture are some very hardworking volunteers at the annual festival. Standing is Lou Carfagno, next to him is Edie Barbone, and seated in front and wearing sunglasses is Nick Barbone. Nick is a regular at the Chance Stand booth the weekend of the event, where for $1 people have the chance to win $5,000. Edie and Lou serve up delicious meatballs. The recipe, of course, for the tasty meat and the sauce is a secret. (Our Lady of Mount Carmel Church.)

Josephine Saccomandi (left) and Sue Piermatteo take a moment to smile for the camera in this 1991 picture taken in the school cafeteria. (Rose Dale.)

In the mid-1990s, Mary Messantonio is in the middle of making hundreds of meatballs in preparation for the annual Mount Carmel feast. Messantonio worked for many years with the feast; Sandy Collins is seen with her back to the camera as she also was part of the food preparation committee. Collins's feast recipes are favorites and in use year after year. (Our Lady of Mount Carmel Church.)

Waiting patiently for the feast crowds are, from left to right, brother and sister Rita and Anthony Chiccino, Nicholas "Ace" Pagano, and Anthony "Chick" Chiccino. Behind the table is the chance ticket basket that holds the many tickets purchased each year by the thousands of feast goers who hope to be the grand prize winner. (Rita Chiccino.)

In this 1981 photograph are some very happy faces as they walk through the feast grounds. People often feel the urge to sing, and most everyone enjoys the spontaneous serenades. Notice the price of soda; according to the sign on the truck behind the entertainers, a cup can be purchased for 15¢. (Jim DeJoseph.)

Crowds gather on the feast grounds in 1973 as everything is in full swing. This scene shows the area behind Our Lady of Mount Carmel Church in Bridgeport. Most years in the past half century have averaged more than 10,000 visitors to the feast during the celebration. What began as a one-day parish procession with picnic to follow has grown to a three-day extravaganza. As long as the weather holds, everyone can count on having a very good time. (Our Lady of Mount Carmel Church.)

Seven

The 2007 Feast

Three beautiful sisters, Victoria, Libbey, and Abbylin Laprise, are getting ready to participate in the 83rd La Grande Festa Italiana. Libbey, who is seven years old and a second-grade Our Lady of Mount Carmel Confraternity of Christian Doctrine (CCD) student, is dressed in the Mount Carmel costume. Victoria is 10 years old and a fifth-grade Our Lady of Mount Carmel CCD student, and Abbylin is one of the youngest participants at only two years old. Flowers are being carried in the procession by all three. (Ginger Laprise.)

Sisters Libbey (center) and Abbylin Laprise (right), along with Sarah Lattanze, walk down Ford Street as the procession festivities begin. Behind the girls are the people carrying the maypole. (Jack Coll.)

It was a beautiful, sunny, but extremely hot day in July. Seen here are the main celebrants of the feast mass held on July 15, 2007: Bishop Daniel E. Thomas, auxiliary bishop of Philadelphia; Rev. Salvatore J. Pronesti, pastor of Our Lady of Mount Carmel; Libbey Laprise, dressed in costume standing next to the bishop; and Sammy Tassoni to the left of Reverend Pronesti. (Ginger Laprise.)

Two-year-old David McNear is seen fishing for prizes at the 2007 Mount Carmel feast. Standing behind David are his mother, Vanessa, his grandmother Vicki Evans, and his father, Vance. The fishing pond is a popular activity for children. (Jack Coll.)

Having a little fun at the fishing pond is three-year-old Ben Chauncey, pulling out a fish in an attempt to win a prize with a little help from his mother, Vicki, as other youngsters look on. The fishing pond gives young children a chance to win a prize with every fish they pull out. (Jack Coll.)

The crowds begin to form outside the church in anticipation of the end of the mass on this very warm Sunday in July 2007. The people who gather waiting for the statues to come out of the church always display expressions of great joy and anticipation. Emotions are visible on the faces of many. For onlookers, it is a very moving experience. (Jack Coll.)

Leading the children in the 2007 procession on Sunday afternoon from left to right are Marion Fortino, nine years old, Maria Fortino, seven years old, and Jillian Speak, nine years old. (Jack Coll.)

Under the direction of Mark DeLuca, the small statue of the patron saint is carried by the children as they begin to make their way on Bush Street. The route of the procession will continue until everyone is back in front of the grotto. The direction has changed many times over the years, but the devotion and determination of the people has not. (Ginger Laprise.)

Patrick Bolognese stands holding the flag outside the San Salvatore Society located on Holstein Street, while waiting for the Our Lady of Mount Carmel Feast procession to begin. His father, Attilio Bolognese, is standing on the steps, and Ricky Falcone is on the right of the photograph. (Attilio Bolognese.)

Members of the San Salvatore Society ("Triple S Club") take a break after marching in the 2007 Our Lady of Mount Carmel procession. Standing outside the society's headquarters on Holstein Street are, from left to right, Jerry Kubrinski, Attilio Bolognese, and Attilio's son, Patrick. (Jack Coll.)

It is an absolutely beautiful day on Ford Street in July as, from left to right, Sal Rotondo, Jon Edwards, Salvatore Barbone, and Nicholas "Chief" Rotondo carry the statue of St. Salvatore held on a wooden carrier. (Jack Coll.)

Seen here are Gina (D'Elia) Virkler standing with Libbey Laprise. Laprise is dressed as the 2007 Our Lady of Mount Carmel. Over 20 years ago, Virkler was the first child to wear this costume in the procession. The costume was made by her mother, who is a descendant of the Romanelli family. (Ginger Laprise.)

It is a family affair in the beer garden at the 2007 feast as family and friends gather to discuss the year's best pork sandwich and meet with old friends. Music was provided by Ten Feet Tall, and the good weather made for heavy crowds. (Jack Coll.)

These young ladies are veteran feast workers and are serving up $4 pork and beef sandwiches at the 2007 feast. Ready to serve are, from left to right, Rose Dale, Julie Barbone, Mary DiSanto, and Philomena Manzo. (Jack Coll.)

Helen Trecroce is all smiles on the right after purchasing her pork sandwiches at the 2007 annual feast. Mary DiSanto stands behind the stand waiting to take care of the next customer. With over 1,400 pounds of pork and 750 pounds of beef sold, there were lots of hungry feast attendees who really enjoyed the sandwiches! (Jack Coll.)

Volunteers from the Bridgeport Elks Lodge 714 spend some time working the Whiskey Wheel at the 2007 feast. Volunteer Elks include, from left to right, Earl Wagner, Ede Kay Biddy, and Mary Morrison; of course, no one under 21 is permitted to play or receive prizes. (Jack Coll.)

It is always a great night out at the annual feast for the Wynne family. Patrick and Rebecca pose on the feast grounds with their six children. The Grove Street residents include, from left to right, Angie, nine years old; Anthony, six years old; and Richie, two years old. Standing in front of his 10-year-old sister Dezzy is Tyler, who is six years old, and Emma is four years old. (Jack Coll.)

Buying T-shirts is a popular event every year at the feast, and working the stand in 2007 are Gina Barbine (left) and Terry Clark. Purchasing T-shirts are sisters Lea DeNaro and Natalie DeNaro (right). (Jack Coll.)

This sausage stand was started back in the 1950s by Vince Giangiulio at the feast before handing the job over to Angelo DeLuca. Angelo talked his sons, Joe and Mark, into doing the cooking. Mark, seen on the far right, has been cooking the sausage for the past 26 years. Mark's son, Anthony, holding a sausage sandwich in the middle, has helped out for more than a decade. Mark's nephew, Angelo, pictured on the left, was happy to participate in this his fourth year at this stand. (Jack Coll.)

Rosemarie Frymoyer knows how to work it, the fried dough roller that is! Frymoyer is a veteran feast worker and has no trouble keeping up with the busy demand for fried dough throughout the feast weekend. (Jack Coll.)

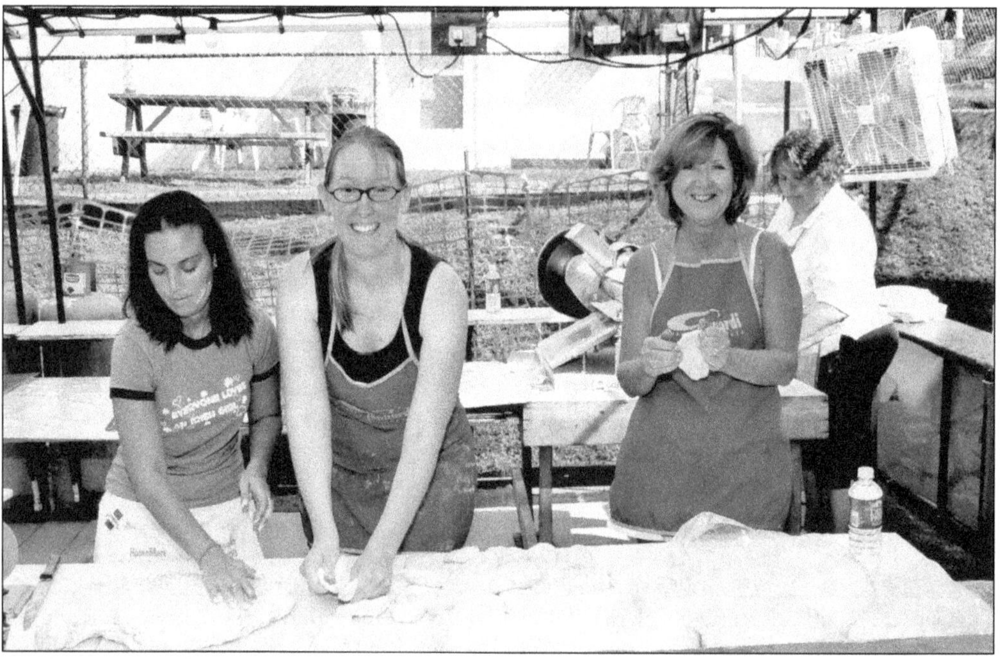

Working the fried dough booth from left to right are Dina DeFrancisco, who has spent many years in this busy stand, and Kris Strouse and Joanne Hannon, both first-year feast volunteers. Fried dough (also known as pizza fritta) is a popular feast treat that attracts long lines every night. (Jack Coll.)

These 2007 visitors to Our Lady of Mount Carmel Feast are all smiles as they enjoy eating and drinking at a makeshift dinner table in the lower parking lot of the church. This happy-looking bunch of festival goers includes, from left to right, Jennifer Early feeding her son Anthony, who was seven months old, as Anthony's sister Annalese looks on. The two youngsters sitting at the top of the photograph are Kayleigh and Kyle Roselands, and to the right is Lisa Roseland holding her one-and-a-half-year-old son Kevin. (Jack Coll.)

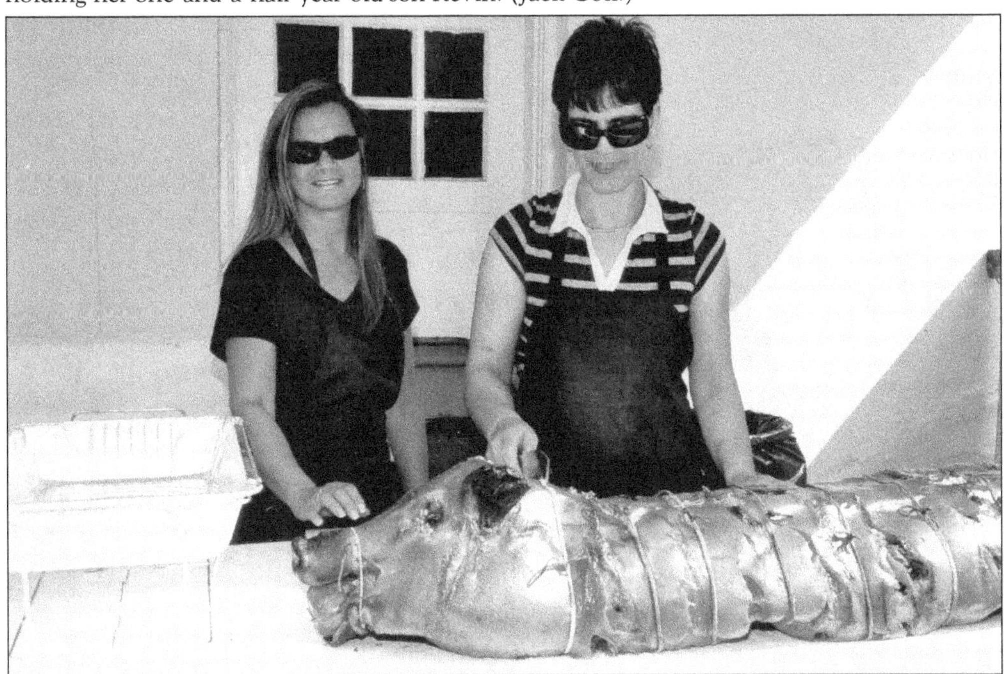
Is there any better sight at the annual Mount Carmel feast than this? The *porchetta* was tender and the lines were long as Rhonda Master (left) and Ikena Gjergo stayed busy day and night carving the pork. (Jack Coll.)

The bleachers provide a perfect place to sit the weekend of the feast and enjoy the entertainment on the Union Avenue stage. Here are father-and-daughter duo Frank and Franny Gentile as they spend some quality time together listening to the Italian melodies of Jerry Trecroce and the band that followed, the Sounds of Jigsaw. (Jack Coll.)

Former Bridgeport mayor Tom Novitski (right) has been a part of Our Lady of Mount Carmel Feast for many years as a volunteer and is seen here handing a soda to Katie and Robert Detrick at the 2007 celebration. (Jack Coll.)

Sisters Josephine Boccella (left) and Theresa DeStefano (second from left) enjoy an afternoon at the 2007 feast. DeStefano is a veteran feast worker. Tracking the food inventory is quite an undertaking during the three-day event, and she was most recently in charge of exactly that. (Jack Coll.)

Pictured here serving up fresh-squeezed lemonade at the 2007 feast are, from left to right, Gabe Pronesti, a 10-year veteran worker at the festival, Rachel Morrison, who has worked the feast for 12 years, as has her mother, Lisa, and her grandparents Lee and Sam Pronesti. Members of this stand are all part of the family of Rev. Salvatore J. Pronesti, Our Lady of Mount Carmel's pastor. (Jack Coll.)

On Sunday, July 15, 2007, following a noontime mass, more than 1,000 residents and parishioners gather outside the church waiting for the annual procession through the streets of Bridgeport to the delight of residents and onlookers. (Jack Coll.)

Three of the hardest-working volunteers at the 2007 annual Mount Carmel feast, according to themselves, include, from left to right, John Santoro, Pat Santoro, and Sal Rotondo. The hardworking threesome is working the beef sandwich booth. (Jack Coll.)

Taking a break from working the dollar store at the annual feast are, from left to right, Marie Royds, Marie Capaldo, and Lorraine Strizziere. Everything at this store offered to perspective customers has been donated by parishioners, as well as friends of Mount Carmel. The many treasures for sale from the stand provide income for parish programs. (Jack Coll.)

Bridgeport residents and parishioners are enjoying themselves on Saturday afternoon at the 2007 feast as they sit in the grandstand enjoying the music of the Verdi Band. The Verdi Band was followed by the sweet sounds of Italian music provided by Nick Desiderio and his band. (Jack Coll.)

Checking in from Collegeville, Pennsylvania, are members of the Maro family at the 2007 feast. Standing behind the baby strollers are Bob and Caryn, 12-month-old Carmine is sitting in the back on the left, joined by her brother, Anthony, sitting in the front and sister, Carmela, on the right. (Jack Coll.)

The feast is a family affair, and residents travel from all over Montgomery County and beyond. The Smith family travels from Royersford every year and is seen enjoying a few good hot dogs. From left to right, members of the Smith family include five-year-old Emily, six-year-old Leah, Darlene, five-year-old William, and Jeff. (Jack Coll.)

Seen here are Maria Russo, Mary Ciaccio, and Chris Rotay, as well as many others as they make their way down Ford Street in the religious procession of the 2007 feast. Many people join together to form a human rosary. Their voices join in prayer as they recite the decades of the rosary and walk the streets that surround the parish grounds. (Jack Coll.)

What a beautiful sunny day it was for the 2007 procession. Nick Ottaviano and his granddaughter Sabrina are anxiously awaiting the signal to begin in procession. Directly behind them are the members of the devotees of the Madonna Grande Society. All are members of the St. Valentine Club, located on Depot Street in Bridgeport. (Our Lady of Mount Carmel Church.)

Debbie Cane and Ralph Colucci are still smiling after working a three-day weekend at the 83rd La Grande Festa Italiana. Cane is the stand coordinator for the water ice booth. Colucci is a veteran sausage stand worker. Colucci also provides a delicious breakfast each year for all the feast workers on Sunday morning of the festival weekend. Both Colucci and Cane represent the true meaning of commitment and dedication to this fine parish tradition. (Charlotte Iannone.)

Many families in town plan picnics at their homes the weekend of the feast. The family of Dennis and Susanna Orangers join at their residence every year for the July festival, and 2007 was no exception. Living on the procession route affords everyone from this group a prime viewing advantage. From left to right are Anna Bonanni, Lucy Bonanni, Tony D'Orsogna, Mary Dell'Arciprete, Ralph Dell'Arciprete, Mary Dell'Arciprete, and Raymond Bonanni. For many of those who come to Bridgeport this weekend in July it is not just about coming to the feast, it is about coming home. (Jack Coll.)

www.ingramcontent.com/pod-product-compliance
Lightning Source LLC
LaVergne TN
LVHW081338110826
845153LV00010B/358

* 9 7 8 1 5 3 1 6 3 6 7 3 9 *